A Simpler Way:

A Practical Guide

To

Home Recording, Mixing, and Mastering

By

Branson M. Smith

ISBN 978-1-365-48300-4

A Simpler Way: A Practical Guide to Home Recording, Mixing, and Mastering

Introduction

First and foremost, I want to state that this work of non-fiction is aimed at the novice/beginner audio engineer. Yes, even if you're new to the world of sound recording, you're still an engineer in some aspect or another.

The book is divided into chapters of five. The first is almost an introductory chapter that helps the reader (you) ease into the gear/equipment and software needed for a home studio. The second focuses on the recording process, the third covers MIDI, the fourth is on mixing, and the fifth is a basic 'how-to' of Mastering from home.

I must also state that I am no professional or expert in the field, but I do have some years of experience. I've taken classes at Del mar College in Corpus Christi and three audio production classes at Full Sail University (online); most of my experience is either from hands-on learning, self-teaching through text books, or tutorial videos via the Internet. I would say from novice to advanced, I would be intermediate, as my knowledge is not vast and my experience is minimal, especially recording drums.

I want to be blunt and honest with the reader in my knowing and experience.

I'm always learning … like you.

Chapter 1: Introducing the equipment

Every home studio will have a different set-up and different equipment, but essentially everything will operate the same.

Overview

First: Most engineers prefer Apple's Mac OS rather than Windows, but it is a preference deal in which OS to run your software and work from.

Next is the DAW (Digital Audio Workstation), which will be your office and your home. Working strictly in the DAW without analogue hardware is called working 'In the Box'.

Finally, the interface, monitors, headphones, and microphones you'll be using. Also, before proceeding, you may be inclined, if you so choose, to use a separate 'Mastering' software.

DAW (Digital Audio Workstation)

The DAW can be used for several things and consists of a variety of features. In Propellerhead's Reason, there is the sequencer, mixer, and rack.; often times, the DAW consists of a library, sequencer, and mixer. The 'workstation' is your 'office' so-to-speak. It's where you'll be working. Here, you will record, mix, edit and, if you wish, master.

Interface

An interface can be defined as what converts analogue sound, via the microphone, and communicates that to the DAW software running on the computer. For a small scale production, a standard 2 channel interface will suffice; however, if recording drums ... 4, 8, or even 16 channels/Inputs may be necessary. The Inputs are versatile. XLR and TRS cables are common cables used between microphones and interface or instruments and interface.

Microphones-Phantom Power (48v)-D.I. (Direct Injection

A microphone can be defined as a transducer that take analogue and turns it into electricity, which in turn become digital.

A 'dynamic microphone' is basically a stage microphone primarily used for 'live' applications. A condenser mic is for studio-use applied to vocals and some instruments. It is more sensitive because of the internal mechanisms, such as its diaphragm … little or big. A dynamic mic, like the Shure 57, can be used on guitar amps and the drum snare. Shure's sm7b is a dynamic microphone that requires 'Phantom power'; condenser mics require phantom power or 48 volts of electricity. Some condenser mics may need a dedicated power supply; in more expensive mics, this is common.

Note: let phantom power (48v) power down before unplugging the mic; if not, the speakers could pop and break.

Microphones have different 'polar patterns', which are the range of the mic, that can be used for different applications. There is omnidirectional, cardioid (unidirectional), super-cardiod, bidirectional (figure-8 pattern), and a variety of microphones come with a switch for multiple patterns.

Besides dynamic and condenser mics, there are ribbon, boundary, contact, and a mic called shotgun.

Other switches besides selecting different polar patterns are 'pad', which controls the output of the mic when recording high levels, and the 'low-cut filter', which ignores any frequencies below a certain point which also is referred to as the 'high-pass filter'.

Microphones, condenser mics specifically, have a variety of diaphragm sizes. Commonly, for drums, two small diaphragm mics that are an identical pair are placed in different pattern shapes (standard left and right, 'X-Y' pattern, etc) are used as 'overhead' for cymbals, but two large diaphragm mics can be substituted as a means to take in the entire drum kit, rather than just the cymbals.

Other than recording with a microphone, there is 'Direct Injection' aka 'D.I.'. Direct means plugging, for example, the electric guitar straight into the interface to record which allows definition and clarity of the instrument; bass guitars are recorded D.I. Interfaces these days most of the time come with direct injection built in.

Monitors & Headphones

Real quick, monitor speakers that are powered are a necessity for playback, and especially in mixing; never mix with headphones on. Headphones, semi-open or closed, are for monitoring purposes only … unless mastering.

Note: never have monitors directly on your desk/workspace surface or against a wall; use monitor stands and form a triangle (3' x 3' x 3') and at head-level.

Controllers, aka digital mixers

Now, for the hands-on engineer, they do offer what is called a 'controller' which is basically a mixing board/interface that runs with your DAW. If you press a button on the controller, for example 'solo', you will 'solo' the track in your DAW software. Different mixers have different features, but the standards are (on each channel) the fader, mute & solo, eq (low, mid, & high), gain, pan, and aux. They offer several Ins & Outs, but sometimes, on smaller surfaces, only allow stereo out (meaning left & right outs). These controllers/interfaces can have built-in effects, but most prefer analogue equipment for added effects such as reverb and delay; the built-in FX are pretty good though.

Aux is for effects and monitoring; it basically sends your signal out, and it's up to the engineer what he/she wants to do with that signal.

Panning is used to create depth and space.

Gain is setting the level.

Eq is to manipulate the frequencies of the signal.

Solo is to listen to a single track.

Mute can be used to single out a track, or, for example, take out the guitars for a moment to hear just bass and drums.

<u>Faders</u> are to mix your tracks.

<u>Preamps</u>

It's common for an interface or a controller to have built-in preamps. A preamp is what allows 'head room' and defines quality of the signal. The better the preamp (and mic), the better your sound will be ... usually. The preamp's quality should be your main concern and most engineers choose to have a separate interface from their pres rather than use the built-in combination. A high-quality preamp can range from a thousand dollars to thousands of dollars, and that's for a single channel ... most of the time.

A 2 channel interface with built-in pres and d.i. will suffice in any production, besides drums. For a full-drum kit, consider a 2 channel interface with an 8 channel preamp combined via optical cables; you'll have 10 channels at your disposal.

<u>The room, acoustics and managing sound</u>

For the home studio, there are many things one can do to manage sound. The whole room doesn't necessarily have to be 'sound proof'; corners are best as well as edges to acoustically treat. Having the desk in the center of the room will help with monitoring. Put acoustic treatment above and at the sides of the desk/work space.

Two rooms are better than one. If a separate room dedicated to recording is available, then that would be the ideal thing; even a vocal booth would help your recordings greatly.

If only one room is available, try not to corner the drums, and higher ceilings are preferred. Don't aim the amp at a solid wall, or have the vocalist sing in to corners or a flat surface.

A recording, mixing engineer's room will be totally different from that of a mastering engineer's. I've read that in a mastering house, you can literally hear your heart beat and feel the throb of it in your ears.

Little things like a pop-filter for vocals, and blankets over amps/mics and drum/mics can assist the home engineer immensely.

Chapter 2: Set-up & the basics of recording

Now that you have an idea of the equipment needed, let's go through setting it up.

First: here's a check list ...

- Computer

- Interface

- Monitors & headphones

- XLR & TRS cables

- Assortment of preferred microphones

Above is the basic set-up for a small-budget home project recording studio. Of course, much more, like analogue equipment and software plug-ins can be added.

DAW set-up

Protools, Cubase, Logic pro (exclusive to Mac), and Propellerhead's Reason are all different digital audio workstations, either is fine although Protools is the industry standar. Most times the software will require an Internet connection and an 'Ignition key'.

Interface

The three common connections to hook-up an interface to a computer are USB, firewire, and thunderbolt (exclusive to Mac). Most times, a 2 channel interface will get its power supply from the computer, but larger interfaces will need to be plugged into a power outlet.

After the DAW is installed and the interface is connected, the monitors and headphones should be next.

For a separate mastering software, it should be installed as well, but will take place much later in production.

For this section, I'll write from the hypothetical stand-point that the engineer is working strictly with a 2 channel interface; an 8 channel interface or more preamps will be for drum recording although it is possible to record an entire kit with '2' mics.

Recording electric guitars

Direct injection is used for definition and clarity while placing a mic to the amp and recording is used for the bottom/low-end frequencies.

Place the mic on the grate of the amp about an inch outside the cone of the speaker. Moving closer and farther from the center of the cone will change the audio. Play with this until you're satisfied with a guitar sound.

For 'direct', an amp simulator can be used; simulated distortion is fine for definition. I've used a clean setting on the sim and ran a distortion pedal with the guitar to get the definition I wanted.

Hint: Adding a hint of delay on the lead guitar can bring out different characteristics.

Acoustic guitar

Use a condenser microphone and place it near the opening of the guitar; different positions will give a variety of sounds and timbre. Changing the polar pattern of the mic can change-up things as well.

Acoustic/Electric guitar

Use 'D.I.' for definition and a condenser mic to get the natural tone of the guitar. With 2 channels, an engineer can record simultaneously.

Bass guitar

The bass guitar is the center-point and starting-point of your mix as I'll present later. D. I. is appropriate here, whether an amp sim is used or multi-effects processor. Some bass amps do have a 'line-out- which can be used to get a preferred bass sound.

Vocals

Record using a phantom powered condenser microphone; investing in a better mic for this application is recommended. Use a pop-filter and keep the mic away from flat surfaces, such as a wall

Recording the drum kit

- The more channels and mics, the better; although 2 mics can be done.

- The kick drum mic an engineer can place outside of the drum head, inside the drum, or have 1 mic on the outside and another mic facing the kick drum beaters. I've seen engineers cover the mic and bass drum with a blanket. Pillows and blankets can be placed into the drum to dampen the tone of the drum which is pretty common I you're having trouble with the timbre.

- For the snare, place a mic, like the 'Shure 57', a few inches away, but pointed towards the middle of the drum; the farther out, the more of a "snap" one will find. A second mic placed beneath the drum can offer more tones to the audio track.

- Left & Right 'over-heads' placed 3' from the kit and 6' apart should be pointed directily at the cymbals. Large diaphragm mics will be directed towards the entire kit; small diaphragms are for precision and to take in the cymbals only.

- Toms & floor tom(s) should be treated like the snare drum

These are the more common set0ups and instruments recorded. Recording is about preference and finding a unique approach. Style and technique define <u>your</u> sound. Positioning, depth, and placement will be your methods.

Chapter 3: MIDI & Programming

MIDI (Musical Instrument Digital Interface) is <u>not</u> an instrument, rather a platform to create music. Most commonly used with a keyboard controller, one can manipulate notes in the DAW's software to effect a virtual instrument's output creating music i.e. "I create this note, the note is played via my virtual guitar sim." If you're without a keyboard controller, often times the software will provide a sim keyboard to notate notes wanted to be written. For instance, on my sim keys, I can use my mouse to enter a 'C' note on my digital interface and that note will be created. However, without a chosen virtual instrument, this is redundant because you will get <u>no</u> sound. MIDI only controls the dictation of notes, it's up to you to use a digital/virtual instrument, such as a synthesizer plug0in, to have playback. The nice thing about creating music with MIDI is that the notes aren't dedicated to that one particular instrument which means you can choose synth, bass, or guitar to playback your written notes. This is ideal for composers and musicians who play guitar, but can't play keys … like me.

I call all of the above programming, which, in a sense, it is. You, like the language of a computer, program the notes in one at a time to dictate the playback of music. I think this is rather cool and handy if you're into synthesizers, oscillators, etc. You could program an entire orchestra if wanted using tools in MIDI such as velocity, volume, and, depending on the instrument, sustain, as well as panning.

I'd like to take this time to talk about virtual drum kits that can be programmed. There are many plug-ins that available to the 'self-recording' musician, who doesn't fancy himself a drummer or lacks the capabilities, such as myself; I can't hold a steady double-kick whatsoever. A virtual kit is also great to have if your client is a fold/singer-songwriter/solo artist and wishes to add drums to their music; I've done this and, as long as they play to a metronome, it sound terrific.

"ive been solo for years now and write/compose with MIDI daily. I often use the Redrum machine in Reason to simulate a drummer; I like fast double-bass and interesting drum fills. Being able to program the kit allows me the freedom to manipulate the rhythm, timbre of sound, and playability of the sim instrument.

I have also programmed guitars, bass guitar, and synth. Reason 8 is dedicated to MIDI technology, synth users, and "In the Box" engineers. Their platform is very user-friendly and intelligent. To simulate a guitar, I created a digital instrument which simulates clean guitars and added an amp sim in the 'FX' library. There, I chose my amp effect (distortion). After opening the MIDI platform, I simply notate the melodies and patterns I desire; bass guitar works the same way.

A rather short chapter, in conclusion, MIDI and the virtual instruments is a very important aspect. Although not recording necessarily, programming is a division of the studio and can be a useful tool.

Chapter 4: A Mixing Mind

- Beginner: The world of recording can be a confusing and overwhelming one. You may ask yourself: where do I begin? What does this do? What's that for? The curiosity that drives you, however, will get you far in your quest for knowledge

The basics: Eq, compression, limiter, and effects (such as reverb and delay). As a beginner, you may not have heard of any of these. If an enthusiast without practice, you may be familiar with each term. These are to be <u>applied</u> to the audio recorded to manipulate the original analogue sound digitally.

Equalization: To enhance, decrease, or omit frequencies within the audio recorded. You may boost the signal, omit frequencies with precision, and take away unwanted 'noise' (such as feedback, hum, fuzz, etc).

Compression: What is it to compress a signal? A compressor, sometimes called a limiter, 'limits' the peak values and compresses them to allow the engineer to boost the gain (volume) without breaking your equipment.

Limiting simply contains the peak values to not exceed passed a set limit

Reverb creates atmosphere (… an echo, if you will) an ambience to the instrument or voice. Added, it can bring out the characteristics of a mundane microphone.

Delay creates a particular repetitive effect simulating the sound multiple times. You may set this at different speads and mix in more or less (dry & wet).

- Intermediate: Knowing is what makes you and expert on a particular subject. Practicing is what makes you a professional. Being both makes you a 'Master of your chosen craft'.

Study frequently the art of sound engineering and you shall flourish as a student, which you will forever be because no one knows it all. Preference and opinion differentiate one engineer from another.

As a mixing engineer, your specialty is … well … mixing. You'll need to know a few basic things after recording about mixing.

1) The bass guitar is King.

2) Kick drum is the Queen.

3) Snare comes after and …

4) Vocals are the last in this 'main mix'; guitars and the rest of the kit will follow and fall neatly into place.

Note: Before mastering, turn down the master fader to -3db, -4db, or -5db, which will allow headroom in your future mastering endeavors.

Before touching faders and panning, let's add a few effects to your recorded audio.

- Reverb for the snare

- Reverb for the enter drum kit

- Delay on the lead guitar

- Delay on solos as well as a dash of rever to add epth

- Compression on the bass guitar

- Delay & Reverb on the vocal track(s)

- Advanced: Eq, faders, panning, and compression

Before adjusting the mix, eq will bring out characteristics of the audio not yet heard.

- Bass guitar: There are several different patterns that can be used.

Example) Boosting +1db-10db at 250Hz and decreasing -1db-10db at 500Hz.

Example) Add a low-cut/high pass filter and cut-off anything below 60-65Hz.

It's not until you get in there and mess around with the eq frequencies that you will find the sweet spot, but for bass guitar, boosting the low-end is key; raising some highs and mids could bring out some 'bite' in the bass ... if that is the sound you desire.

I mentioned compression on the bass earlier. Let's take a moment to learn how to properly compress audio.

- Ratio control – 2:1, 4:1, and 8:1 are common
- Threshold – at what signal peak you wish to compress/limit
- Attack & Release – controls the signal envelope
- Gain-reduction – shows and controls the amount of compression
- Knee – determines the quickness of the compression.

Attack should be slow, the release should be fast, and threshold should be set high. Start with the threshold by decreasing until you see compression happening. Turn the attack faster until the instrument's characteristics change, then slow it a bit ot not over do it. Now, tweak the release until a desired volume is reached.

The compression covered above is for general use; I thought I'd go over it sooner than later.

I believe I covered panning in the first chapter, but I'll reiterate in a basic layout before moving onto the other instruments and vocals.

- Bass stays in the middle
- Kick stays in the middle along with the Snare
- Lead guitar – I like to pan far Right – Left or Right
- Rhythm guitar – far Right or Left, opposite of other guitar
- Keys/synth/effects are preference, but keep from panning too far right or left
- Over-heads – one left and one right – stereo pair (exact make and model; twins)
- Tom 1 can be panned left a bit
- Tom 2 panned right a bit
- Floor tome can be panned more right (…this will add a flow from left to right [a tom roll will sound more interesting])

- Vocals (main) stay in the middle

- Backing vocals are a preference

Note: Remember – Eq, mix fadrs, eq again. In mastering, it would be: compression, eq, and compress again.

I'm not going to dive too much into equalizing each instrument and vocal, but the purpose is to bring out the best of each audio track recorded.

Overall, the procedure should be in mixing as follows:

- Bass at -3db

- Mix to preference

- Eq each track

- Mix again

- Pan

- Maybe mix again

- Your effects

- Mix

- Check Eq

- Mix once more

...that should suffice.

Chapter 5: The how-to of a basic master

"Mastering" can be defined as the final formatting of an audio track, album, or project. It is <u>not</u> making the audio sound 'prestine', although that is a result.

We're going to stay "In the box" for this, but most professional mastering engineers use an analogue mastering chain to work though along with their computer and different software.

Your tools:

- Compression

- Equalization

- Limiters

- Stereo Imager

- Maximizer

Different software will vary, but these are the basics – especially compression/limiting & EQ.

Mastering is a lot like mixing. Here is the procedure:

- -3db on the Master fader before bouncing the track to an audio file (bouncing is exporting)
- Import that audio file back into your preferred DAW or separate dedicated mastering software
- Compression
- EQ
- Reverb (to past everything together)
- Compression once more
- Check EQ

Reason 8 offers a maximizer and stero imager which is great to utilize.

Basically, your increasing the input and output, manipulating the audio characteristics, and trying to get it crystal-clear (a home studio <u>can not</u> compete with a professionally built studio or its analogue mixing desks/consoles; you can get pretty close though to a product you'll be proud of.

I would go more in depth, but there are literally books on the market that are 250+ pages on just the subject of mastering. In fact, there are text books dedicated to just recording, just mixing, and primarily focused on mastering; I'd suggest reading up on each subject.

I, myself, am still learning the techniques of mastering so not to steer you in the wrong direction, I'll end the chapter by saying if you're not confident to 'master' your recordings, then hire a professional who does it on a daily basis. If you strive, like me, to be a well-rounded engineer, then knowledge is key to your success in pursuing being a decent to great recording, mixing, and mastering engineer.

Chapter 6: Concluding the Practical Guide

I hope with this guide I've properly taught you how to set-up your gear, how to record audio, mix the tracks, and start at the beginning of mastering. If I have failed to do so, questions and/or comments are always welcome via my official website.

I hope I've taught you the basics and I have helped you to spread your engineering wings – so to speak – a bit.

www.ingramcontent.com/pod-product-compliance
Lightning Source LLC
Chambersburg PA
CBHW021852170526
45157CB00006B/2406